DAS F-PRINZIP®

BY FEYYAZ

EDITION A|2007

0831/2000

DAS F-PRINZIP – a pleasant acquaintance

I remember that evening well – a genial bunch of people at a friend's.

It was lying on a sideboard and as soon as I discovered it, my attention wandered from the conversation to the contents of the simple cardboard box. I saw the pieces lying there and immediately began to handle them.

Everything fitted perfectly and one could almost arbitrarily make up combinations by piling the pieces or placing them next to each other. From simple figures to complex structures – everything was possible. The boldest assemblages also had a tendency toward the fragile, unstable.

Then I started thinking about the number of possible combinations and trying them one after the other... didn't I just have that combination or was it a mirrored version?
Short notes on a napkin helped, but it was still difficult to fathom.

In categories, according to typology with two, three, four, on top of each other, next to one another, interlocked... the possibilities are manifold.

4 simple wooden elements in the form of an "F" – with a pleasant smooth surface made of wood, a natural product in perfect precision.

The creation of sculptural work with modular elements is one of the things that my colleagues and I are faced with on a daily basis.

This, in turn, originates incessantly new forms which are reminiscent of well-known symbols. Since our student days we have time and again introduced so-called "alphabet-cities" into our projects!

Urban blocks turned into objects thanks to openings on the side are readable from the air. The thought of a European city with its traditionally closed building blocks benefits greatly in real life from openings such as gaps or courtyard entries.
Even landmarks of architectural history ranging from El Lissitzky's *Wolkenbügel* to Steven Holl's beautifully sculptural competition entries from the 80's are reflected in these objects.

DAS F-PRINZIP stands for all of these – or so I thought!

Later I met Feyyaz, the father of the "F-PRINZIP" who has a much freer, profounder view of his work. And now my children are playing with the "F-PRINZIP" and they, too, keep making interesting discoveries.

Peter Berner
KCAP / ASTOC Architects & Planners

DAS F-PRINZIP – eine angenehme Bekanntschaft

Ich kann mich noch gut an den Abend erinnern – eine gesellige Runde bei guten Freunden.

Es lag auf dem Sideboard und kaum hatte ich es entdeckt, verlagerte sich meine Aufmerksamkeit umgehend von der Gesprächsrunde weg, hin zum Inhalt des schlichten Pappkartons. Ich sah sie darin liegen und begann unmittelbar damit zu hantieren.

Alles passte gut zueinander und ließ sich beinahe beliebig an-, auf-, neben-, über-, und untereinander kombinieren. Von einfachen Figuren bis zu komplexen Skulpturen war beinahe alles möglich. Die gewagtesten Kombinationen hatten aber auch den Hang zum Fragilen bis Unstabilen.

Dann begann ich über die potentielle Anzahl der Kombinationen nachzudenken und diese Stück für Stück auszuprobieren ... hatte ich diese Kombination nun schon, oder war es die gespiegelte Variante?
Kleine Notizen auf der Serviette halfen mir, aber es war nicht wirklich genau zu ergründen.

In Kategorien, nach Typologien, mit Zwei, Drei, Vier, aufeinander, nebeneinander, ineinander ... die Möglichkeiten sind mannigfaltig.

4 einfache Holzelemente in "F" Form – mit angenehmer, glatter Oberfläche aus schönem Holz, ein Naturprodukt in perfekter Präzision.

Die Möglichkeiten mit modularen Elementen skulptural zu arbeiten beschäftigen meine Kollegen und mich tagtäglich bei unserem Tun.

Dabei entstehen immer wieder Formen, die Nähe zu bekannten Symbolen haben. Schon seit unseren Studienzeiten haben wir immer wieder gerne so genannte "Alphabet-Cities" in unsere Projekte eingebaut!

Städtische Blöcke die durch Öffnungen in den Flügeln zu Objekten werden und aus der Luft gesehen sogar lesbar sind. Der Gedanke der Europäischen Stadt mit ihren traditionell geschlossenen Baublöcken bereichert sich im wirklichen Leben durch Öffnungen wie z.B. Baulücken oder Hofeingänge.
Auch Landmarken der Architekturgeschichte von El Lissitzky's *Wolkenbügel* bis hin zu Steven Holl's wunderbar skulpturalen Wettbewerbsentwürfen aus den 80ern, spiegeln sich in den Objekten wieder.

Für all diese Dinge steht DAS F-PRINZIP – dachte ich!

Später habe ich dann Feyyaz, den Vater des "F-PRINZIP" kennengelernt, der eine viel freiere, weiterführende Sicht auf sein Werk hat. Und nun spielen meine Kinder mit dem "F-PRINZIP" und auch sie entdecken ständig noch Neues.

Peter Berner
KCAP / ASTOC Architects & Planners

DAS F-PRINZIP – un agradable encuentro

Todavía me acuerdo bien de aquella noche – una agradable reunión de buenos amigos.

Estaba en el estante y apenas la descubrí mi atención se desvió de las conversaciones comunes para centrarse en el contenido de la sencilla caja de cartón. Las vi allí dentro e inmediatamente empecé a manipularlas.

Todas encajaban y casi se dejaban combinar a voluntad entre sí, unas junto a otras, unas encima y debajo de otras. Prácticamente, todo era posible, desde sencillas figuras hasta complejas esculturas. Sin embargo las combinaciones más audaces tenían también tendencia a la fragilidad y la inestabilidad

Luego empecé a pensar en la cantidad potencial de combinaciones y me dediqué a probarlas una a una... ¿Me había salido ya esta combinación, o era la variante en sentido contrario?
Pequeñas anotaciones en una servilleta me servían de ayuda, pero realmente no lo podía averiguar con exactitud.

En categorías, según tipologías, con dos, tres, cuatro, una encima de otra, una junto a otra, una dentro de otra...las posibilidades son múltiples.

4 simples elementos de madera en forma de „F" – con una agradable superficie lisa, de hermosa madera, un producto natural en perfecta precisión.

Las posibilidades de trabajar esculturalmente con elementos modulares es algo que nos ocupa a mis compañeros y a mí en nuestro quehacer diario.

Así surgen continuamente formas que se aproximan a símbolos conocidos. ¡Ya en nuestros tiempos de estudiantes nos gustaba incorporar a nuestros proyectos una y otra vez las llamadas "Ciudades alfabeto"!

Bloques urbanos que con aberturas en sus alas se convierten en objetos e incluso se pueden leer desde el aire. La idea de la ciudad europea con sus tradicionales bloques de edificios cerrados se enriquece en la vida real con aberturas como p. ej. solares vacíos o entradas de patios.
En los objetos se reflejan también hitos de la historia de la arquitectura desde el *Wolkenbügel* (Nube de Hierro) de El Lissitzky, hasta los proyectos de concurso maravillosamente esculturales que realizara Steven Holl en los años 1980.

¡Para todas estas cosas existe DAS F-PRINZIP! – pensé yo.

Más tarde conocí a Feyyaz, el padre del „F-PRINZIP", quien tiene una visión mucho más libre y amplia de su trabajo. Y ahora son mis hijos los que juegan con el „F-PRINZIP" y también ellos descubren constantemente algo nuevo.

Peter Berner
KCAP / ASTOC Architects & Planners

DAS F-PRINZIP – une agréable découverte

Je me rappelle encore cette soirée – une excellente compagnie chez de bons amis.

L'objet reposait sur le buffet et à peine l'eus-je découvert que mon attention se détourna aussitôt de la conversation pour se concentrer sur le contenu de ce simple carton. Je les voyais reposer à l'intérieur et commençai tout de suite à les manipuler.

Toutes les combinaisons semblaient possibles : contre, dessus, à côté, par-dessus et dessous. Des figures simples aux sculptures complexes, presque tout était réalisable. Cependant, les combinaisons les plus hardies tendaient aussi vers le fragile, jusqu'à l'instable.

Je commençai ensuite à songer au nombre potentiel des combinaisons et à les essayer, l'une après l'autre…avais-je déjà celle-ci ou n'était-ce que son reflet ?
De petites notes sur ma serviette m'aidaient, mais il n'était pas vraiment possible de déterminer ce nombre exact.

Les possibilités abondent… par catégories, selon des typologies, par deux, trois ou quatre, les uns sur les autres, côte à côte, les uns dans les autres.

4 éléments simples en bois, en forme de « F » – dotés de la surface agréable et lisse d'une belle essence, un produit de la nature d'une précision parfaite.

Mes collègues et moi-même réfléchissons tous les jours, tout en vaquant à nos occupations, aux possibilités de travailler de façon sculpturale avec des éléments modulaires.

Ce faisant, nous créons des formes proches de symboles connus. Depuis nos études, nous avons toujours intégré volontiers à nos projets lesdites « Alphabet-Cities ».

Les blocs urbains qui, grâce aux ouvertures des ailes, deviennent des objets et, en vue aérienne, sont même lisibles. L'idée de la ville européenne avec ses îlots traditionnellement fermés s'enrichit dans la vie réelle d'ouvertures telles que les territoires vacants ou les entrées de cour.
Certains grands repères de l'histoire de l'architecture se reflètent dans ces objets, du *Wolkenbügel* d'El Lissitzky aux projets merveilleusement sculpturaux que Steven Holl réalisa pour des concours dans les années 1980.

DAS F-PRINZIP s'applique à toutes ces choses – ainsi pensais-je !

Plus tard, j'ai fait la connaissance de Feyyaz, le père du « F-PRINZIP », qui a une vision beaucoup plus libre et stimulante de son uvre. Aujourd'hui, mes enfants jouent avec le « F-PRINZIP » et eux aussi découvrent sans cesse quelque chose de nouveau.

Peter Berner
KCAP / ASTOC Architects & Planners

DAS F-PRINZIP – un piacevole incontro

Mi ricordo ancora bene di quella sera, in buona compagnia a casa di amici.

Stava sulla credenza e non appena la scorsi, la mia attenzione si spostò immediatamente dalla conversazione al contenuto di quella semplice scatola di cartone. La vidi là dentro e cominciai subito a giocherellarci.

Tutto combaciava perfettamente e si lasciava combinare in successione, di sopra, di fianco, di sotto, quasi a completo piacimento. Dalle figure più semplici alle sculture complicate, era praticamente tutto possibile. Le combinazioni più audaci, però, tendevano ad essere fragili e instabili.

Quindi cominciai a riflettere sul numero potenziale delle combinazioni, provandole una dopo l'altra... questa l'avevo già tentata o si tratta della sua variazione riflessa?
Mi aiutavo con piccoli appunti presi sul tovagliolo di carta, e tuttavia non riuscivo a capire del tutto.

Per categorie, per tipologie, a due, a tre, a quattro, una sull'altra, una a fianco all'altra, una dentro l'altra... le possibilità sono molteplici.

Quattro semplici elementi a forma di "F", dalla superficie liscia e gradevole di bel legno, un prodotto naturale dalla precisione perfetta.

Ogni giorno io e i miei colleghi siamo alle prese con le opportunità che scaturiscono dalla lavorazione sculturale degli elementi modulari.

È così che continuano a nascere forme che si avvicinano a simboli noti. È da quando eravamo studenti che ci piace inserire delle cosiddette "Città Alfabeto" nei nostri progetti!

Isolati urbani che diventano oggetti grazie alle aperture nelle ali e che, per di più, visti dall'alto risultano leggibili. Il concetto europeo di città con i suoi isolati tradizionalmente chiusi, nella vita reale si arricchisce di spazi aperti, come per esempio le porzioni di terreno non edificate o le entrate ai cortili. In questi oggetti si riflettono inoltre anche alcuni dei simboli paesaggistici della storia dell'architettura, dal *Wolkenbügel* di El Lissitzky fino ai progetti per concorso degli anni '80 splendidamente sculturei di Steven Holl.

DAS F-PRINZIP, pensavo, significa tutte queste cose!

Più tardi conobbi Feyyaz, il padre del "F-PRINZIP", il quale guarda alla sua opera con sguardo molto più libero e ampio. E ora i miei figli giocano con dell'"F-PRINZIP" e anche loro fanno continuamente nuove scoperte.

Peter Berner
KCAP / ASTOC Architects & Planners

ty of possible combinations. The artist Feyyaz has liberated the first letter of his name from its original purpose already many years ago and introduced it to a new world of horizon-expanding abstraction. To imply a purely coincidental and therefore arbitrary alliterative inevitability would be quite wrong as the F – and anybody is free to test the truth of this statement – has far greater constructive potential than any other letter of our alphabet. And since man, at least modern man, has always valued the principle, the serial and the modular, he is incessantly engaged in a quest for sources of systematic deductions of this kind which he attempts to justify in technical, historical, philosophical, symbolical and – naturally - esthetic terms. However, few who have tackled this have been as unencumbered and so willing to make statements as Feyyaz. How can a circle, square or even a Corbusierian modular compare to a perfectly proportioned F? Those who start playing with these attractive wooden Fs will soon realize that there is no real comparison – and reminisce about happy hours spent as a child playing with building blocks.

Hier wird der Buchstabe F zum Prinzip erhoben, zu einer modularen Konstruktionsfigur, die mit ihrer unvermuteten Vielzahl kombinatorischer Möglichkeiten zu beeindrucken weiß. Der Künstler Feyyaz hat den Anfangsbuchstaben seines Namens schon vor vielen Jahren von seiner eigentlichen Bestimmung befreit und der blickweitenden Abstraktion zugeführt. Nun aber eine ausschließlich zufällige und damit beliebige alliteratorische Zwangsläufigkeit zu unterstellen, wäre ganz falsch, denn das F birgt – für jeden überprüfbar – weit größere konstruktive Potentiale als alle anderen Buchstaben unseres Alphabets. Und da der Mensch, zumindest der Mensch der Moderne, das Prinzipielle, Serielle und Modulare besonders schätzt, forscht er immer wieder nach Quellen für systemische Ableitungen dieser Art, die er technisch, historisch, philosophisch, symbolisch und natürlich ästhetisch zu begründen sucht. So unbelastet und setzungsfreudig wie Feyyaz haben bisher allerdings wenige auf diesem Gebiet gehandelt. Was ist schon ein Kreis oder ein Quadrat oder ein Corbusier'scher Modulor gegen ein perfekt proportioniertes F. Wer mit diesen schönen hölzernen Fs zu spielen beginnt, wird das schnell feststellen – und sich gerne an die glücklichen Stunden erinnern, die er als Kind mit Bauklötzen verbracht hat.

Aquí se eleva la letra F a la categoría de principio, a la de figura de construcción modular, que impresiona con su inusitada cantidad de posibilidades combinatorias. Hace ya muchos años que el artista Feyyaz ha liberado la inicial de su nombre de su propia determinación y ha alimentado la abstracción amplia. Ahora bien atribuirle una obligatoriedad exclusivamente casual y con ello arbitrariamente aleatoria, sería completamente incorrecto, ya que la F esconde – todo el mundo lo puede comprobar – un potencial constructivo mucho mayor que cualquier otra letra de nuestro alfabeto. Y como el ser humano, o al menos el moderno, aprecia especialmente los principios, las series y los módulos, investiga pues constantemente las fuentes de este tipo de deducciones sistémicas, para las que busca razones técnicas, históricas, filosóficas y, naturalmente, estéticas. Sin embargo hasta ahora pocos han procedido en este terreno como Feyyaz, de una forma tan libre de gravamen y a la vez entusiasta. ¿Qué es un círculo o un cuadrado, o incluso un modulor de Le Corbusier en comparación con una F perfectamente proporcionada? Quien empiece a jugar con estas bonitas efes de madera lo comprobará enseguida – y se acordará con gusto de las horas felices que pasó de niño jugando con los bloques de construcción.

La lettre F est érigée ici en principe, en figure de construction modulaire, qui ne manque pas d'impressionner par le nombre insoupçonné de ses combinaisons possibles. Voici déjà de nombreuses années, l'artiste Feyyaz a libéré l'initiale de son nom de sa vocation et l'a portée vers une abstraction qui élargit le regard. Cela dit, il serait tout à fait erroné de n'y voir qu'une nécessité aléatoire et de ce fait facultative, découlant d'une allitération, car le F renferme – ce que chacun peut vérifier – des potentiels conceptuels nettement supérieurs à ceux des autres lettres de notre alphabet. Et puisque l'homme, du moins l'homme moderne, apprécie particulièrement ce qui est relatif au principe, à la série et au modulaire, il cherche sans cesse des sources de déductions systémiques de cette sorte, qu'il tente de justifier aux plans technique, historique, philosophique, symbolique et naturellement esthétique. Du reste, jusqu'à maintenant, peu sont intervenus sur ce terrain avec un esprit aussi libre que Feyyaz et un tel désir de présenter les choses. Qu'est-ce donc qu'un cercle ou un carré ou le Modulor de Corbusier par rapport à un F aux proportions parfaites ? Tous ceux qui commencent à jouer avec ces beaux F en bois le constateront vite – et se rappelleront volontiers les moments heureux passés avec leurs cubes dans leur enfance.

Qui la lettera F viene elevata a principio, a figura della costruzione modulare che sorprende per la sua poliedricità inattesa in quanto a possibilità di combinazione. L'artista Feyyaz già da molti anni ha svincolato la lettera iniziale del suo nome dalla sua determinazione propria portandola ad una astrazione lungimirante. Eppure sarebbe del tutto sbagliato presupporre una inevitabilità esclusivamente casuale (e con questo una qualsivoglia inevitabilità allitteratoria) poiché la F nasconde – e chiunque lo può verificare – potenziali costruttivi molto più ampi di tutte le altre lettere del nostro alfabeto. E dal momento che l'uomo (perlomeno l'uomo dell'età moderna) apprezza ciò che è principiale, seriale e modulare, egli è costantemente alla ricerca di fonti di deduzioni sistemiche di questo genere, che cerca di motivare dal punto di vista tecnico, storico, filosofico, simbolico, e, naturalmente, estetico. Tuttavia, finora sono in pochi ad essersi avventurati su questo terreno nel modo spensierato e piacevole in cui l'ha fatto Feyyaz. Cosa è mai un cerchio, un quadrato o un Modulor di Le Corbusier in confronto a una F perfettamente proporzionata? Chi comincia a giocare con queste belle F di legno se ne accorgerà immediatamente – e gli tornerà alla mente il dolce ricordo delle ore che da bambino trascorreva giocando alle costruzioni.

Kay von Keitz

DAS F-PRINZIP

A wonderful tool for exploring spatial relationships.

The player is trying to reconcile the proportion between solid and void using a form which is normally linked with language.

In experimenting with the 4 forms the "in between" spaces have an enormous power, they possess an imperfection in proportion which one tries to resolve by rearranging them again.

The proportion of the short bar of the F not being in the middle of the vertical causes a wonderful imbalance which the players try to rectify. The irritation of not being able to find a certain preconceived order encourages the player to continue and to generate more compositions, each having their own reason.

The blocks have no scale. Are we building a city or producing an urban composition? When a composition is achieved the observer can imagine navigating between a series of spatial sequences, possibly a dynamic housing project influenced by Russian constructivism.

The composition can be a soft seating VIP lounge area in a club on which to relax and have a drink incorporating display and information elements, as in a trade fair stand.

The interpretations are dependent on the imagination and perception of the player. A discovery of a new aspect of sensory perception is possible with "F-PRINZIP" shapes.

In arranging the shapes to form the perfect, or more interestingly, the imperfect composition, the player is observing the conflict and struggle all designers go through to solve the fundamental issues of spatial design.

Stephen Williams
STEPHEN WILLIAMS ARCHITECTS

DAS F-PRINZIP

Ein phantastisches Spielzeug, um räumliche Bezüge zu erkunden.

Der Spieler versucht, die Proportionen zwischen fester Masse und leerem Raum aufeinander abzustimmen, indem er eine Form benutzt, die normalerweise mit Sprache in Verbindung gebracht wird.

Experimentiert man mit den 4 Formen, stellt man fest, dass die "Zwischenräume" eine unglaubliche Macht haben, sie besitzen eine proportionale Imperfektion, die man durch ständiges Umarrangieren aufzulösen versucht.

Die Tatsache, dass sich der kurze F-Strich proportional nicht in der Mitte der Vertikale befindet, führt zu einem wunderbaren Ungleichgewicht, das der Spieler auszugleichen versucht. Man ist irritiert, weil man keine vorgegebene Ordnung entdecken kann, wird so aber auch ermutigt, weiter zu auszuprobieren und bringt auf diese Weise ständig neue Kompositionen hervor. Jede davon hat ihren eigenen Anlass.

Die Blöcke weisen keine Maßstäbe auf – bauen wir jetzt eigentlich eine Stadt, entwickeln wir eine urbane Komposition. Sobald ein Arrangement fertig ist, kann sich der Beobachter ausmalen, wie er zwischen einer Reihe von räumlichen Sequenzen gedanklich hin und her pendelt, vielleicht einem dynamischen Wohnungsprojekt, das durch den russischen Konstruktivismus beeinflusst wurde.

Die Komposition könnte vielleicht eine Sitzgruppe in einer VIP-Lounge in einem Club darstellen, wo man sich entspannt und etwas trinkt, wobei Elemente für Display und Informationen integriert sind – wie an einem Messestand.

Wie man das Ganze interpretiert, hängt von der jeweiligen Vorstellungskraft und Auffassungsgabe des Spielers ab. Mit den Formen des "F-PRINZIP" entdeckt man eine neue Dimension sinnlicher Wahrnehmung.

Indem der Spieler die Formen so arrangiert, dass sie eine perfekte oder besser noch eine imperfekte Komposition ergeben, lernt er die Problematik und den Kampf aller Designer kennen, die sich der fundamentalen Schwierigkeit stellen müssen, eine gute Lösung für ein räumliches Konzept zu finden.

Stephen Williams
STEPHEN WILLIAMS ARCHITECTS

DAS F-PRINZIP

Un juego perfecto para explorar relaciones espaciales.

El jugador intenta compaginar la proporción entre la materia sólida y los espacios vacíos utilizando una forma que normalmente está unida al lenguaje.

Al experimentar con las 4 formas de los "espacios intermedios" se obtiene un poder increíble, ya que éstas poseen una imperfección proporcional que se trata de zanjar reacomodándolas.

La proporción del trazo corto de la F que no está en el medio de la vertical provoca un desequilibrio que el jugador intenta rectificar. El fastidio de no ser capaz de encontrar un orden preconcebido impulsa al jugador a continuar y a generar más composiciones. Cada una de las cuales tiene su propio sentido.

Los bloques no tienen ningún patrón, son como edificios formando una composición urbana. Cuando la edificación está conseguida, el observador se puede imaginar navegando entre una serie de secuencias espaciales, posiblemente un proyecto urbano influenciado por el constructivismo ruso.

La composición puede representar un salón VIP en un club, con un display y algunos elementos informativos, donde uno se relaja y se toma una copa, asícomo el stand de una feria.

Las interpretaciones dependen de la imaginación y la percepción del jugador. Con las formas del "F-PRINZIP" es posible descubrir un nuevo aspecto sensorial.

Llas formas se acomodan para crear la composición perfecta, o mejor aún, la imperfecta. El jugador observa y, de esta forma, conoce el conflicto y los problemas a los que se enfrentan los diseñadores para encontrar una solución plausible a los conceptos dimensionales.

Stephen Williams
STEPHEN WILLIAMS ARCHITECTS

DAS F-PRINZIP

Un outil merveilleux pour explorer les relations spatiales.

L'acteur tente de réconcilier la proportion entre solide et vide en utilisant une forme qui est habituellement liée au langage.

Les expériences sur les 4 formes révèlent le pouvoir considérable des espaces « interstitiels », qui possèdent une imperfection de proportion que l'on essaie de résoudre en les agençant de nouveau.

La barre courte du F, n'étant pas au milieu de la verticale, provoque un merveilleux déséquilibre que l'acteur cherche à rectifier. L'irritation de ne pas parvenir à trouver un certain ordre préconçu l'encourage à continuer et à générer davantage de compositions. Chacune ayant sa propre raison.

Les blocs sont dépourvus d'échelle – construisons-nous vraiment une ville, créons-nous une composition urbaine ? Lorsque l'on parvient à une composition, le spectateur peut imaginer naviguer entre une série de séquences spatiales, peut-être une cité dynamique inspirée du constructivisme russe.

La composition pourrait être les sièges d'un salon pour VIP, avec écrans et éléments d'information, dans un club où l'on peut se détendre et boire un verre, comme sur le stand d'un salon professionnel.

Les interprétations dépendent de l'imagination et de la perception de l'acteur. Les formes du « F-PRINZIP » permettent de découvrir une nouvelle dimension de la perception sensorielle.

En agençant les formes pour créer la composition parfaite ou, ce qui est plus intéressant, la composition imparfaite. L'acteur observe le conflit et la lutte qu'affrontent tous les concepteurs pour résoudre les problèmes fondamentaux de la création en trois dimensions.

Stephen Williams
STEPHEN WILLIAMS ARCHITECTS

DAS F-PRINZIP

Uno strumento splendido per esplorare le relazioni spaziali.

Chi ci gioca cerca di conciliare la proporzione fra pieno e vuoto usando una figura normalmente collegata alla lingua.

Nelle sperimentazioni con le quattro parti di questa figura, gli spazi che si creano tra esse hanno un potere enorme; in loro è insita un'imperfezione di proporzioni che si cerca di risolvere attraverso una nuova disposizione.

Il fatto che la stanghetta più corta della F non si trova al centro di quella verticale provoca un meraviglioso squilibrio, cui tenta di mettere rimedio la persona che ci gioca. Il disappunto provocato dall'impossibilità di rintracciare un certo ordine preconcetto invoglia il giocatore a continuare a creare nuove composizioni, ciascuna con un suo proprio significato.

Gli elementi non sono in scala. Sono edifici cittadini o stiamo creando una composizione urbana? Quando si ottiene una composizione, l'osservatore può immaginare di muoversi attraverso una serie di sequenze spaziali simili a un progetto dinamico di edilizia residenziale influenzato dal costruttivismo russo.

La composizione può essere un soffice divano nella sala VIP di un locale dove ci si potrebbe accomodare e rilassarsi bevendo qualcosa mentre si ricevono informazioni, come ad esempio in uno stand fieristico.

Le interpretazioni dipendono dall'immaginazione e dalle percezioni di chi gioca. Con le forme dell'"F-PRINZIP" si può scoprire un nuovo aspetto della percezione sensoriale.

Nell'accostare le forme per creare la composizione perfetta, o ancora meglio, quella imperfetta, colui che gioca si rende conto dei conflitti e dei dubbi cui ogni progettista deve far fronte per dare una risposta alle questioni fondamentali del design tridimensionale.

Stephen Williams
STEPHEN WILLIAMS ARCHITECTS

DAS F-PRINZIP

The letter takes on form,
surface takes on volume,
two-dimensionality becomes three-dimensionality
the immaterial becomes material.

stacked,
interlocked,
piled,
intertwined,
juxtaposed,
layered,
turned.

Many things are possible, yet left open.
The play on forms is impulse, inspiration and model - its aim is to develop this thought and become architecture.

DAS F-PRINZIP

Der Buchstabe wird Form,
Die Fläche zum Raum,
zweidimensional wird dreidimensional,
Immaterielles materiell.

gestapelt,
verzahnt,
übereinander getürmt,
ineinander geschoben,
nebeneinander,
geschichtet,
verdreht.

Vieles ist möglich und bleibt doch offen.
Das Spiel der Formen ist Anstoß, Inspiration und Skizze, dies weiterzudenken und Architektur zu werden.

DAS F-PRINZIP

La letra se convierte en forma,
La superficie en espacio,
lo bidimensional se convierte en tridimensional,
lo inmaterial en material.

amontonado,
encajado,
apilado uno sobre otro,
introducido uno dentro de otro,
uno junto a otro,
estratificado,
retorcido.

Mucho es posible y sin embargo queda pendiente.
El juego de las formas es iniciativa, inspiración y boceto, seguir pensando en esto y convertirse en arquitectura.

DAS F-PRINZIP

La lettre devient forme,
La surface espace,
le bidimensionnel se fait tridimensionnel,
L'immatériel, matériel.

Empilés,
imbriqués,
entassés les uns sur les autres,
poussés les uns dans les autres,
côte à côte,
stratifiés,
distordus.

Les possibilités, immenses, restent pourtant en suspens.
Le jeu des formes est impulsion, inspiration et esquisse, pour penser plus en avant tout cela et le faire devenir architecture.

DAS F-PRINZIP

La lettera diventa forma,
La superficie spazio,
le due dimensioni diventano tre,
l'immateriale si fa materiale.

Sovrapposti,
interconnessi,
gli uni sopra gli altri,
gli uni accanto agli altri,
stratificati,
distorti.

Esistono molte possibilità, ma non tutte sono realizzabili.
Il gioco delle forme è impulso, ispirazione e abbozzo, per continuare a pensarci e trasformarlo in architettura.

Imke Haasler
DELUGAN MEISSL ASSOCIATED ARCHITECTS

Biography

DAS F-PRINZIP is created by the artist Feyyaz. It is the result of the constant development of his own artistic work. This 3D board game concept is based on a constellation of four equally formed F-shapes modelled on the walls of a rectangular room. Purpose of the game is to explore the manifold, sheer endless possibilities of creating floor plans and three-dimensional constructions.
As a connector between language, shape and function, DAS F-PRINZIP enhances spatial thinking and compacts the idea of space into a recurring principle with numerous variants.

1962	born in Istanbul, Turkey
since 1969	living in Cologne, Germany
1985-1992	Academy of Arts, Cologne
since 1992	media and concept artist
since 2003	creative director for daab publishing

Together with the publisher Ralf Daab, Feyyaz developed a new, trendy and unique program of design, architecture and photography books.

Acknowledgements

Thanks to my friend Ralf Daab for his trust in my work - and for his confidence in entering a new exciting world beside books.
A special thanks to Peter Berner, KCAP/ASTOC Architects & Planners, for enthusiastically refining and finalizing the F-shapes.
Thanks to Nicole Rankers for her great support in developing DAS F-PRINZIP as a fine product.
Many thanks to Karsten Thormaehlen for taking the photographs of DAS F-PRINZIP.
Thanks to Peter Berner, Stephen Williams, Kay von Keitz and Imke Haasler for their wonderful texts.

FORM FOLLOWS FUNCTION FREEDOM ...

© 2007 daab
cologne london new york

published and distributed worldwide by
daab gmbh
friesenstr. 50
d-50670 köln

p +49-221-913 927 0
f +49-221-913 927 20

mail@daab-online.com
www.daab-online.com

publisher ralf daab
rdaab@daab-online.com

creative director & editor feyyaz
DAS F-PRINZIP and the logo are registered trademarks of feyyaz
© 2006-2007 by courtesy of feyyaz. all rights reserved.
mail@feyyaz.com

© texts by peter berner, stephen williams
kay von keitz and imke hassler
© all images DAS F-PRINZIP by karsten thormaehlen
© portrait of feyyaz by emil zander

translations
english ingo wagener
german mechthild barth
spanish concepción dueso
french virginie de bermond-gettle
italian graziano pintus
translations and copy-editing durante & zoratti, cologne

printed in china

isbn 978-3-937718-91-0

all rights reserved.
no part of this publication may be reproduced in any manner.